@RosenTeenTalk

Life Skills

T0282132

PREPARING FOR COLLEGE IRL

Elissa Bongiorno

ROSEN
PUBLISHING

Published in 2025 by The Rosen Publishing Group, Inc.
2544 Clinton Street, Buffalo, NY 14224

First Edition

Editor: Greg Roza
Designer: Rachel Rising

Photo Credits: Cover, pp. 1, 3, 5, 45 pics five/Shutterstock.com; Cover Cosmic_Design/Shutterstock.com; Cover, pp. 1, 3–48 Vitya_M/Shutterstock.com; pp. 3, 15 Ground Picture/Shutterstock.com; pp. 3, 25 Rawpixel.com/Shutterstock.com; pp. 3, 33 Jacob Lund/Shutterstock.com; p. 7 ImageFlow/Shutterstock.com; pp. 9, 11 Monkey Business Images/Shutterstock.com; p. 13 Gorodenkoff/Shutterstock.com; p. 17 M_Agency/Shutterstock.com; p. 18 garagestock/Shutterstock.com; p. 19 oneinchpunch/Shutterstock.com; p. 21 CarlosBarquero/Shutterstock.com; p. 22 BRO.vector/Shutterstock.com; p. 23 ARMMY PICCA/Shutterstock.com; p. 24 Darko 1981/Shutterstock.com; p. 27 Ground Picture/Shutterstock.com; p. 28 AMV_80/Shutterstock.com; p. 29 haireena/Shutterstock.com; p. 31 David A Litman/Shutterstock.com; p. 34 Andrii Symonenko/Shutterstock.com; p. 35 Vixit/Shutterstock.com; p. 37 Pheelings media/Shutterstock.com; p. 39 thodonal88/Shutterstock.com; p. 40 Sertaki/Shutterstock.com; p. 41 PeopleImages.com - Yuri A/Shutterstock.com; p. 42 maybeiii/Shutterstock.com.

Some of the images in this book illustrate individuals who are models. The depictions do not imply actual situations or events.

Library of Congress Cataloging-in-Publication Data

Names: Bongiorno, Elissa, author.
Title: Preparing for college IRL / Elissa Bongiorno.
Other titles: Preparing for college in real life
Description: [Buffalo] : Rosen Publishing, [2025] | Series: @RosenTeenTalk.
   Life skills | Includes index.
Identifiers: LCCN 2024008037 (print) | LCCN 2024008038 (ebook) | ISBN
   9781499477573 (library binding) | ISBN 9781499477566 (paperback) | ISBN
   9781499477580 (ebook)
Subjects: LCSH: College student orientation--United States--Juvenile
   literature. | College choice--United States--Juvenile literature.
Classification: LCC LB2343.32 .B66 2025 (print) | LCC LB2343.32 (ebook) |
   DDC 378.1/98--dc23/eng/20240314
LC record available at https://lccn.loc.gov/2024008037
LC ebook record available at https://lccn.loc.gov/2024008038

Manufactured in the United States of America

CPSIA Compliance Information: Batch #CSRYA25. For Further Information contact Rosen Publishing at 1-800-237-9932.

Find us on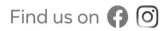

CONTENTS

Chapter 1

What Do You Want to Do When You Grow Up?

"You should be thinking about college."

This is all I hear. From teachers! My parents! I mean, I want to go to college and all. But it's so much work!

I'll have to figure out where to apply. I've been searching online. Looking at colleges. I'm not sure of how far from home I'd like to go. The idea of **dorm** living is exciting but scary. But I'd miss Mom, Dad, and my little sister Kayla. I made an appointment to talk with my **guidance counselor**. I know I need to think about what I want to do with my life. My strengths and weaknesses.

Then there's the **applications**. And the personal statement!

There's so much to think about. I'm not sure how to get started. It's frustrating!

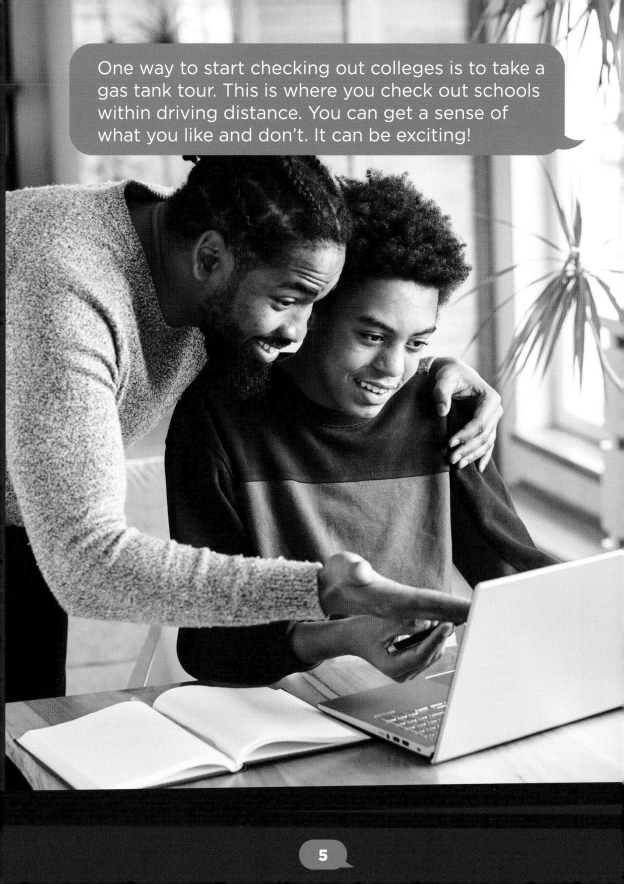

One way to start checking out colleges is to take a gas tank tour. This is where you check out schools within driving distance. You can get a sense of what you like and don't. It can be exciting!

CONSIDERING CAREERS

Your mom is a doctor. Your grandpa was a plumber. Your dad is an artist who works from home. There are so many career options, or choices. It's good to have some ideas about your future career, or job. This will help with your college search.

Ask Yourself
- What do you like to do?
- What are you good at?
- What do your friends and family think you are good at?

Check It Out
- Talk to people in careers you're interested in.
- Search careers online.
- Find out the salaries (pay) and time commitments.

Career Quiz

- Not sure about a career path? There are many **aptitude** tests you can take. Ask your guidance counselor. Or try some online quizzes. These can help you think about options. You can learn more about your skills and what you are good at.

When thinking about a career, consider what is important to you. Salary? Creativity? Support? Time off? There are so many things to consider.

WHO DO YOU KNOW?

Teens can **network**, too. For example, do you want to work in a hair salon? Ask your parents and your friends if they know anyone who is in that business. Make connections. Find out about careers right from the source.

YOUR HIGH SCHOOL COUNSELOR

Now that you're thinking about college, it's time to talk to your high school counselor. You might meet one-on-one, or in a small group. Either is great! Here are some questions to ask:

- What classes should I be taking?
- What colleges do students from our school attend?
- What schools do you think might be right for me?
- Do you have any handouts I should look at?

Your counselor knows a lot about applying to college. If there's something you want to know, just ask! They can help.

Your counselor may have a lot of students to help. Be prepared for your meetings. Show up early. Bring your questions. This way you can get all the information you need.

DIFFERENT CAREER PATHS

Different jobs require different schooling. There are options after you finish high school. It all depends on what you want to do as a career. If you would like to keep going to school, you have options!

	Community College	Public University
Degree	**Associate's degree**	**Bachelor's degree**
Time	two years	four years
Average Cost per Year	$3,990	$11,260
Careers	nursing assistant, carpenter, mechanic	scientist, engineer, teacher
What Else?	close to home, costs less	campus life, freedom

Get Your Hands Dirty

Do you like working with your hands? Here are some jobs to consider.

- computer repair person
- medical tools repair person
- X-ray **technician**
- aircraft mechanic

Do you like cars? Planes? Motorcycles? You could work as a mechanic. Check out community college options. There are jobs out there for you.

TWO + TWO

Sometimes students begin at a community college. Then they transfer, or switch, to a four-year university. They can live at home for longer. Their schooling can cost less. But you need to research both schools! This is because classes you take at one school might not count at another school. If transferring, make sure the classes you take will be accepted.

COURSE OF STUDY

Now you have a sense of some career paths. Time to think about what courses, or classes, you need to take. Talk with your counselor. Look up **requirements** at schools you like. Here's what to think about:

1. You need to **graduate** high school! Make sure you meet your high school's rules for graduating.
2. Generally, you will need to take classes in:
   a. English
   b. math
   c. history
   d. science
   e. foreign language (usually a language other than English)
3. Electives: These are classes you can take in all different subjects. Try art. Tennis. Psychology. This is a good chance to find out what interests you.

AP Classes

Advanced Placement classes allow you to take college classes in high school. Your school may offer different AP classes such as English, biology, or chemistry. You can find out more about AP classes at **apstudents.collegeboard.org**

AP classes have exams, or tests, at the end of the year. If you get a high score, you can earn college **credit**. Students study hard all year to do well.

WORD UP

Your GPA is your "grade point average." It's an average of all your grades. Honors and AP classes can count more.

Grade	Points
A	4
B	3
C	2
D	1
F	0

Chapter 2

LET'S GET READY

You might have heard people talking about extracurricular activities. These are things you do aside from taking classes. They can be fun! But also, they can help you get into college. Here are some examples:

- sports
- model United Nations
- drama/theater
- orchestra/band/chorus
- student newspaper
- blog or vlog
- community service
- after school job

There's no need to do every activity. Think about what you are interested in. Pick a few. Try them out. If a club does not exist, why not start it? Talk to your teachers.

Mix It Up

Like soccer and singing? Colleges like that too! Some experts say having a mix of activities, like sports and music, can be especially appealing to colleges.

Consider leading. Start your own club. Or, after a few years, get to be the president or team captain. This is a great way to show off your leadership skills to colleges.

BE CONSISTENT

Once you find an activity you like, keep going. Participate for several years. This shows commitment, or the ability to keep a promise to do something. You can have fun and impress colleges at the same time!

HOW DO YOU SPEND YOUR SUMMER?

You can think about possible careers and find a way to try them out. Here are two important examples:

Volunteering

Volunteering means doing something without expecting to be paid for it. Helping others can help you too. You can learn about your community. You will meet people different from you.

- **Animal Lover?** Help out at a local animal shelter. You can walk dogs, play with them, and clean cages.
- **Love Teaching?** Ask at school if you can be a tutor, or a one-on-one teacher. Younger students may need your help!
- **Interested in Medicine?** Check out your local hospital. Many have volunteer programs.

Working

Another way to spend your summer is working. You can earn money, learn new skills, and make friends! Start by looking online. Ask your family and friends. Be careful not to commit to too many hours, though. Not all jobs need to be a path to a career. Here are some good jobs for teens:

- babysitter
- cashier
- lifeguard
- dog walker
- server
- lawn mower

Volunteering benefits everyone, and helps you get into college? Check out the following links to learn more about volunteering opportunities near you.

- www.redcross.org/volunteer/volunteer-opportunities.html
- www.volunteer.gov

INTERNSHIPS: TRYING OUT CAREERS

A great way to discover what you want to do is to try it out! This is what internships are for. But how do you find one?

- **Network.** Ask friends and family. Do they know someone in the field you want to try? See if they'll introduce you to someone willing to help you.
- **Online Search.** Check the internet for internships. (Always run results by an adult!)
- **Ask in School.** Your teachers or guidance counselor may know of opportunities. Ask them!

INTERNSHIP

Like What?

Stumped? Not sure what type of internship to look for? How about:

- **Love animals?** Ask at a zoo, veterinarian's office, or animal shelter.
- **Love STEM?** Check out **architecture** companies, tech companies, and science museums.
- **Love writing?** Visit a newspaper, publisher, public relations firm, or radio station.

Some internships pay you. Others do not. You need to decide if the opportunity is worth the time and effort. Your family and guidance counselor can help you make the best decision for you.

WORKING WORLD

When it's time to start your internship, act professionally. This means you should be on time. Dress appropriately. Always be polite. Be helpful. Do your work as asked. Don't forget to ask questions! You are there to learn.

My Internship Starts Today!

I'm so excited! I'm so nervous! Today I start my internship.

I really love math. My aunt is an accountant. She found out about an internship program. I applied and got in! Now for eight weeks, I'm working at an accounting firm. I can't believe it.

I'm wearing a blazer. I keep tugging at the sleeves. But I know I need to dress professionally. My aunt told me all about office attire. My dad took me shopping.

I get *my own desk*. I sit with a bunch of accountants. I hope I make friends. I try to keep track of everyone's names. I really want to do a good job. I know these connections can help me later. It's actually been kind of fun. I'm on my way!

Thank you notes are important. Write one after your interview. Write several after your internship. Thank people who helped you. They will be glad to know they were **appreciated**.

KEEPING TRACK

You're having lots of experiences: extracurricular activities, volunteering, work, and internships. That means you need to keep track. Make yourself a **résumé** to list and display your experiences.

Education: List schools attended, dates, GPA, special classes.

Work and Volunteer: List positions, dates, short descriptions of what you did.

Awards: Be sure to list any awards you have won and include dates and details.

Skills: Do you know how to write computer code? Do you speak more than one language? Do you have CPR training? Add it here!

Use active verbs to describe yourself and make your résumé pop. It will sound more powerful. Try words like: created, coached, solved, shaped, guided, and examined.

Chapter 3

TIME TO RESEARCH

There are so many colleges out there. Which ones should you apply to? Start by making a list. How? With research!

Here are four main topics to consider when researching colleges:

Location: How far do you want to be from home? Do you want to live in a dorm?

Size: Think about your high school. Would you like to attend a college that's bigger? Smaller? The same?

Academics: What subjects would you like to study? What schools offer those subjects?

Cost: Check out the tuition.

Keeping Track

Take notes as you research schools. You can do this in a notebook or create a **spreadsheet**. Keep track of location, tuition, and student body size. Research the classes offered, sports played, and dorm options. This will help you decide what schools to apply to when you are ready.

You can use this website from the U.S. Department of Education to look up schools: **nces.ed.gov/collegenavigator/** You can search by location, major, degree, and much more.

TALK TO PEOPLE

A great way to find out about a college is to talk to alumni, or people who already graduated from the college. They can tell you what the school is really like. Ask those in professions you are interested in, too. Want to be a lawyer? Ask one where they went to school.

COLLEGE FAIR FUN

A college fair is a great place to learn about many colleges at once. Generally, schools will each have a booth with a representative or two. You can talk to them. Here are some tips:

Think Ahead. Beforehand, make a list of what schools you want to check out.

Dress the Part. Wear clean, neat clothes. Look nice!

Ask Great Questions. What programs are most popular? What type of students are happiest? Again, think ahead to plan what you want to ask.

Collect Contact Information. Get a business card from the representative. If you liked the school, follow up with a thank you note.

Some college fairs are virtual, or online. This is a great option to check out a lot of schools from home. Prepare as if you were attending in person. And make sure you aren't in your PJs!

MONEY, MONEY, MONEY

College can cost a lot of money. It's important to face these costs head on. Don't hide! Here's how to start:

Talk with Family: Ask your parents or guardians if they can help pay. It might feel awkward, but it's important to know.

Figure Out the Real Cost: Tuition is not the only cost of college. Buying books, for example, is something you will need to do every semester. If you will live away from home, you must pay for a room and food.

Scholarships

Scholarships can help you pay for school. They provide money you do not have to pay back. There are many types of scholarships. Some are local. Some are by interest. Use the same tools you did to find schools to find scholarships: internet searching, networking, asking your guidance counselor. Then get to applying!

Sometimes you can get money for college through work study. This is a program where you work on campus and get paid. Only certain students qualify. It depends on your FAFSA application.

FREE APPLICATION FOR FEDERAL STUDENT AID (FAFSA)

This is the starting point to getting money to attend college. You can apply beginning October 1 of the year before you will go to school. Just remember that you need to pay off school loans after you graduate. You can find the form here: **www.usa.gov/fafsa** (Learn more about financial aid in Chapter 4.)

Take a Tour

I looked around the group. I couldn't believe it. I was on a college campus. On a tour. My stomach felt weird and wobbly. It was pretty neat to hear from an actual student. She led us through campus. Everyone was whispering and pointing at buildings. I needed to pay attention. And ask questions. I took a deep breath and raised my hand.

"What do you do for fun here?"

The guide stopped and smiled at me. "Great question. During football season I go to the games. In the winter, there's a coffee house with great music. I'll point it out."

I smiled. My mom patted me on the back. I closed my eyes and imagined myself here, enjoying a football game with new friends. A college student.

Wander! Once the tour is done, walk around some more. Take note of what the guide told you. Then, with an adult, look around more. Use a map and check out the campus for yourself. Get a feel for the place.

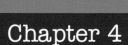

Chapter 4

READY, SET, APPLY

The summer before your senior year can be fun! It's also time to prepare to apply to college. Make a list of schools. Include different types:

Type	GPA of Accepted Students	Acceptance Rate
safety	lower than yours	high (above 40 percent)
match	similar to yours	30 percent or above
dream	higher than yours	low (below 30 percent)

Schools that have low acceptance rates are dream schools for everyone. You might not get in, even if you qualify. This is because so many students apply and there are so few spots.

Other Considerations

- **standardized test** scores of accepted students (if required)
- location
- tuition
- dorm life
- majors
- what you thought of the tour

These ideas will help you build a great list. Think broadly about where you might be happy attending college. You might surprise yourself.

How many schools should you apply to? Applications cost money and require work! Experts suggest applying to between five and eight schools. Use a mix of dream, match, and safety schools.

Don't count out a school just because you might consider it a "safety." It could be a great fit for you! A school does not have to be hard to get into to be awesome.

TESTING, TESTING

Some schools will require you to take standardized tests. They look at your score when you apply. Study before you take them. There are classes and study books. The tests include:

TOEFL: Test of English as a Foreign Language. This test is for those who those who do not speak English as their first language.

SAT: Aptitude test. It has sections on reading, writing, language, and math.

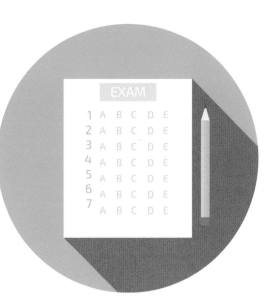

ACT: School-based test. It's more focused on the subject matter you have learned and has sections on reading, English, math, and science.

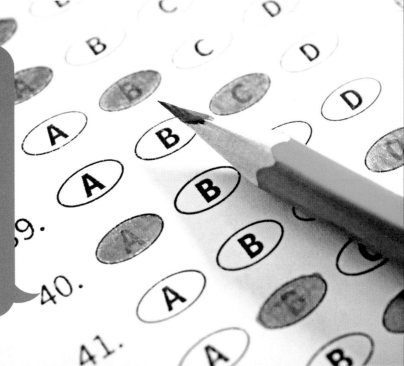

Some schools are test optional. This means you can take the standardized tests if you wish. Submit your scores if they are good. This can help your application, but you are not required to take the tests.

TEST BLIND

Many colleges no longer require standardized tests. This is for many reasons:

Racial Equity: Test questions were deemed to be **biased**. They were easier to answer if you were white. This was unfair to students who identify as other races.

Success Rates: Studies found that the tests do not measure your success accurately. The scores do not predict how you will do in college.

More than 1,900 colleges no longer ask for these tests. Check what the schools you want to apply to require.

LET'S GET PERSONAL

Your personal essay, or statement, is an important part of your college application. It gives admissions officers a chance to know you. Here are some tips:

Be Specific. Take one thing that makes you special. Try writing about that. A secret recipe with your grandma. A dog you cared for who meant a lot. Be creative.

Be Brief. Your essay can be up to 650 words.

Give Yourself Time. Plan to write more than one draft. Start the summer before senior year. This way you won't be rushed.

Stuck? Ask your family and friends for ideas. You don't need to write about a major achievement. Or a giant setback. Write about you. You'll do great!

Why You?

You are more than your GPA or a list of activities. Try to explain this in your college essay. Let the college know why you will be a good student. Show the school how they will benefit from you being there.

A great way to check your work is to read it out loud. You can hear mistakes. You can tell what parts are great. Read your essay to yourself or to your parents or friends. It will make a big difference.

FINDING OUT ABOUT FAFSA

FAFSA can help you pay for college. Here is what you need to fill it out:

1. your **Social Security** number (If you don't have one, that's okay.)
2. your parent's information
   a. full name
   b. Social Security number (if they have one)
   c. mailing address and email address
3. financial information
   a. tax return
   b. checking and savings account
   c. stocks and bonds
   d. real estate
4. list of schools (up to 20 schools you are applying to)

You must fill out the FAFSA form every year you are in college. Keep your information handy. Stay organized. This way it won't be hard to fill it out. You will get the hang of it!

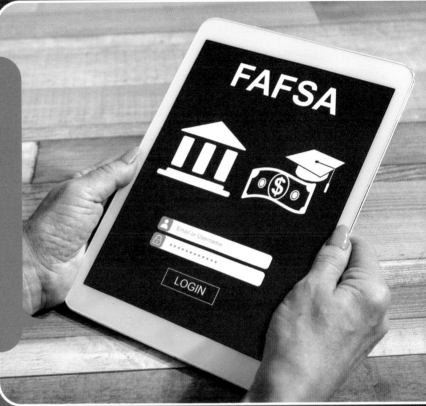

QUICK QUESTIONS

Who? If your parents are divorced, the parent who makes more money will provide their details. If you need more info, visit: **studentaid.gov.**

What? FAFSA is the first step to financial aid. This can be a grant, a loan, or a work study placement—all types of money to help you pay for college. The money can come from the federal government, the state government, or your school.

When? The FAFSA window closes June 30, but the sooner you fill it out, the better.

WHO DO YOU KNOW?

To apply to college, you probably need recommendations. These are letters written by your school counselor and teachers. Think about the people you have a good relationship with. Whose class have you enjoyed? You can ask them! Be sure to make it easy for them.

- Ask early. Give them at least one month to write their letter.
- Provide your grades. Give them a copy of your **transcript**.
- Provide your info. Remember that student résumé you put together? Give them a copy! It will help them write a great letter.

Remember to say thank you. Recommendations take time! Your teachers and counselors are busy, but they want to help you too. And be sure to check back in. Let them know what school you are attending. They'll appreciate it!

SO, YOU WANT A SCHOLARSHIP

Scholarships are money given to you to pay for school. You do not have to pay it back. Types include:

- **Merit Based:** Applicants meet certain requirements, such as a high GPA.

Don't give up! Once you are enrolled in college, you can still apply for scholarships. Ask your college's financial aid office. They might have ideas. Search online. You never know what you'll find!

- **Financial Need:** Applicants show monetary need.
- **Identity Focused:** Applicants match a certain description, such as race, gender, or culture. And much more!

Tips on Applying for Scholarships

Start early. The earlier the better. This gives you time to prepare.

Pay attention. Be mindful of submission details. You don't want to lose out because of a small mistake.

Apply widely. Try for a wide range of scholarships so you have more chances.

WHERE TO LOOK?

There are many online databases to search for scholarships. You should also check with your guidance counselor and teachers. Ask friends and family. Make sure to apply for local scholarships, too. Fewer people may apply. This will give you a better chance! Remember to only apply to scholarships you are qualified for. You don't want to waste time.

I Did It!

I raced home from school. I didn't want to open the email until I was with my dad. We'd worked so hard together to get ready. Tours. Personal essay. The SAT. Recommendations. It hadn't been easy! We had some tough talks about money. About me being far away. But then we decided on a list together. And today was the day. My first-choice school sent out its emails.

"You're going to do great no matter what," Dad told me. I'd gotten into my safety school last month. I still hadn't heard from my reach school. It didn't matter. This was the school I wanted to go to. The one I could afford. The one with the graphic design program.

We held hands.

I clicked open.

I made it in!

Applying to college takes time, patience, and work. But you can do it! Start early and stay focused. You will do great.

GLOSSARY

application: A form one fills out to get something.

appreciate: To understand the worth or importance of something or someone.

aptitude: The ability to learn.

architecture: The art or science of designing and building structures, especially ones that can be lived in.

bias: An attitude that always favors one way of feeling or acting over any other.

credit: Points earned in college for each class a student passes.

dorm: An on-campus living space.

graduate: To successfully finish a course of study; to finish school.

guidance counselor: A person who gives help and advice to students about educational and personal decisions.

network: A group of people one knows and can rely on for help or guidance.

requirement: Something that is necessary to do in order to reach a goal.

résumé: A list of accomplishments to share with employers when applying for a job.

Social Security: A U.S. government program established in 1935 that workers pay into. People receive Social Security funds after a certain age.

spreadsheet: A computer program that allows users to enter information in columns and rows.

standardized test: A test that requires all test takers to answer the same questions. The results allow schools to compare students or groups of students.

technician: Someone experienced with specific technology and tools.

transcript: An official copy of a student's educational record.

INDEX